You Can Be a
Nature
Detective

Peggy Kochanoff

Mountain Press Publishing Company
Missoula, Montana
2009

Dedicated to my family for their support—
even when I was collecting skulls and "poop."

Many thanks to Avai and her magic typing fingers.

Thanks also to Jim Wolford (retired biology teacher at
Acadia University, N.S.) for checking my facts and wording.

Fourth Printing, August 2015

Library of Congress Cataloging-in-Publication Data

Kochanoff, Peggy, 1943–
  You can be a nature detective / Peggy Kochanoff.
    p. cm.
  Includes bibliographical references.
  ISBN 978-0-87842-556-3 (pbk. : alk. paper)
  1. Nature study—Juvenile literature. I. Title.
  QH53.K63 2009
  508—dc22

                        2009004534

PRINTED IN HONG KONG BY MANTEC PRODUCTION COMPANY

MP Mountain Press
PUBLISHING COMPANY
P.O. Box 2399 • Missoula, MT 59806 • 406-728-1900
800-234-5308 • info@mtnpress.com
www.mountain-press.com

Preface

When I was young, my friends and I spent hours playing in the woods, chasing bugs in the fields, catching frogs, searching tide pools, and climbing trees. We didn't realize it at the time, but we were bonding with nature. We were experiencing the fascination, excitement, and joy to be found in nature—not to mention getting physical activity. I am afraid that kids (and some adults) today are disconnected from the outdoors. Without this bond, people are far more likely to pollute, ruin the environment, and allow the extinction of certain plants and animals.

I hope this book can stimulate new interest in nature. There are clues for solving nature mysteries. Who was here, who made that sound, what is that smell, how does that happen? Solve the mysteries and realize how wonderful nature is. Enjoy and protect it!

Look, listen, touch, smell!

Hmmm . . . There's spit all over the grass.

Who could have done it?

Let's look closely and find out.

It's the spittlebug! *Brush some of the spittle off a grass stem and take a closer look. Hiding inside the spittle is the nymph (young) of the froghopper insect. A mother froghopper lays eggs in the plant tissue. When a nymph, or young spittlebug, hatches from an egg in the spring, it sucks the plant juices. The spittlebug passes liquid out its back end and blows air into it, making it foamy. Then the spittlebug hides inside the foam, safe from enemies, the sun, dryness, and temperature extremes. Isn't that amazing?*

 **Mystery solved!**

The adult is called a froghopper because it easily hops like a frog from plant to plant. A froghopper can jump a hundred times its body length!

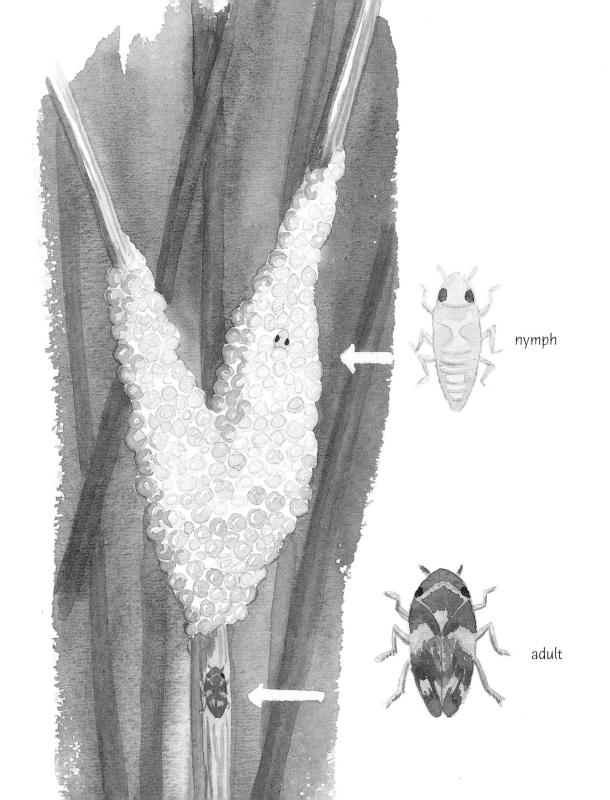

nymph

adult

Hmmm . . . The autumn leaves are turning colors.

Why is that happening?
Let's look closely
and find out.

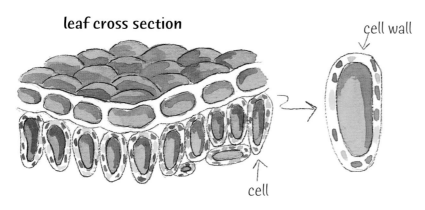

leaf cross section

cell wall

cell

The leaves actually have had yellow and orange pigments all along, but a green pigment called chlorophyll was hiding the other colors during the growing season. Chlorophyll is needed for photosynthesis, the amazing process by which green plants manufacture food. Through photosynthesis, chlorophyll combines the energy of the sun with water and carbon dioxide to form oxygen and simple sugars.

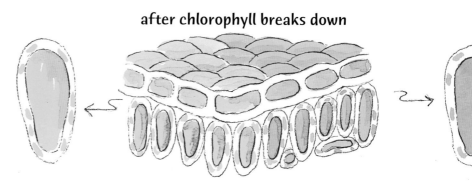

after chlorophyll breaks down

As days get shorter and temperatures drop, trees need to shed leaves to conserve moisture during harsh weather. A barrier of corky cells forms where the leaf stem joins the twig, stopping the flow of moisture and nutrients to the leaf. Once deprived of nutrients, the leaf can no longer make chlorophyll, and the remaining chlorophyll breaks down and disappears. Then the yellow and orange pigments, which don't break down as fast as the green, become visible.

vacuole filled with fluid

anthocyanin pigment

chlorophyll breaking down

The color red comes from the pigment anthocyanin. Levels of anthocyanin in the leaves may increase as the tree prepares for winter.

The final color of any leaf is brown; the color comes from tannins, which are chemicals stored in leaves and bark. Tannins are visible only when the other pigments are gone.

Mystery solved!

Hmmm . . .
Something is calling
in the dark.

tch

trill, trill

jug-o-rum, jug-o-rum

snore,

jingle, jingle

12

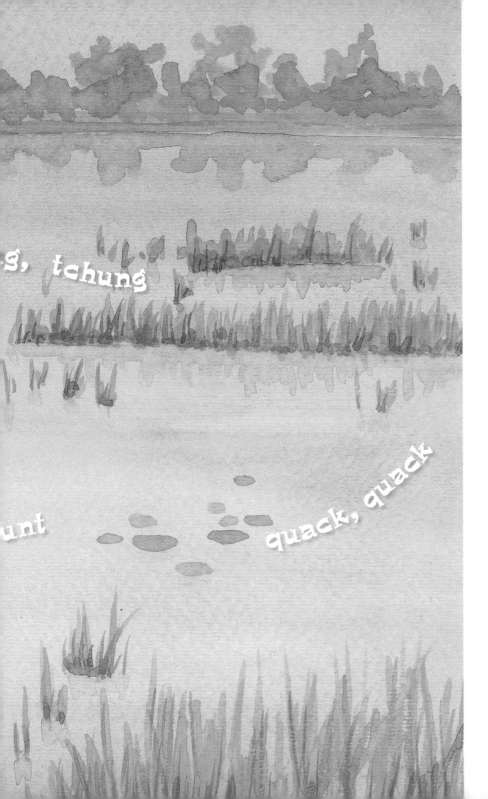

g, tchung

unt

quack, quack

How can you tell which frog or toad it is?

Let's listen closely and find out.

13

American toad

*The bumps on its skin secrete a toxic fluid but don't cause warts and aren't poisonous to human touch. This toad's call is a **musical trill** lasting up to thirty seconds.*

Spring peeper

*One of the smallest frogs (under $1\frac{1}{4}$ inches) in eastern North America. Has a dark X on its back. The call is a bell-like sound (**jingle, jingle**) that carries a long distance.*

Bullfrog

*North America's largest frog (up to 8 inches); usually drab green. The call is a booming **jug-o-rum**.*

Wood frog

It has light brown skin with a dark mask over the eyes. The call is a short, hoarse **quack**, **quack**.

Green frog

Its color varies from green to brown with dark patches. A raised ridge runs along each side of the body. The call sounds like the twang of a loose banjo string: **tchung, tchung**.

Leopard frog

It has circular spots with light borders. The call is a **rattling snore** *followed by* **chuckling grunts**.

Mystery solved!

Hmmm . . .
There's a
caterpillar.

16

How can you tell which moth or butterfly it will become?

Let's look closely and find out.

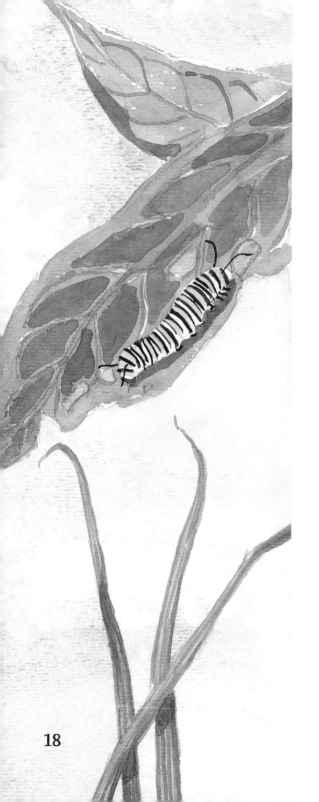

Caterpillars are the larvae (young) of butterflies or moths; the larval stage is the life stage that does almost all of the growing. As soon as caterpillars hatch from their eggs, they start eating (sometimes more than 25,000 times their body weight). In order to grow, a caterpillar usually sheds its skin four times. Most caterpillars are unique, so you should be able to tell which butterfly or moth they will become as adults by the way they look. Another clue is what type of plant you find them on.

Cabbage butterfly

This caterpillar is skinny and green with a faint yellow stripe on top and yellow dashes running along each side. True to its name, it is usually found on cabbage, broccoli, cauliflower, and mustard family plants.

Tomato hornworm

This caterpillar is easy to spot by the harmless horn on its back end. It grows up to be a five-spotted hawkmoth. It's found mainly on tomato plants but also on peppers, eggplants, potatoes, tobacco, and some weeds.

Woolly bear caterpillar

This is an easy-to-recognize, fuzzy, black and reddish brown caterpillar. It likes dandelions, low grasses, and weeds. It grows up to be the Isabella tiger moth.

Mourning cloak butterfly

This caterpillar is mostly dark (as if in mourning). It likes elms, willows, and poplars.

20

Sulphur butterfly

This skinny green caterpillar is similar to the cabbage butterfly caterpillar but has only one yellow stripe on each side. It likes clover and alfalfa.

Monarch butterfly

This caterpillar looks like striped candy and feeds on milkweed.

White admiral

This caterpillar looks like bird poop. It likes willows, birch, and poplars.

Tiger swallowtail

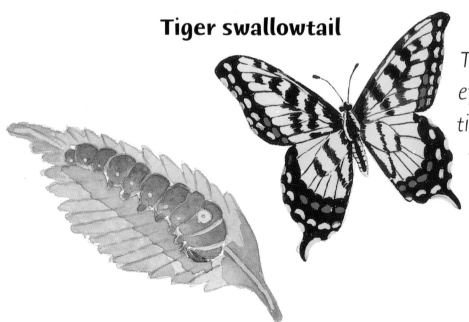

This caterpillar has two large eyespots (remember eye of a tiger) and likes a variety of trees and shrubs.

Painted lady

This caterpillar can be a variety of colors. It has black-tipped, branching spines (think small paintbrushes). It's found at over a hundred plants but favors thistle.

Cecropia moth

With its spikes and knobs, this caterpillar looks "creepy" (remember cecropia). It likes various trees and shrubs.

Mystery solved!

Hmmm . . . There's a terrible smell.

What could it be?
Let's sniff
closely and
find out.

Skunk

You or your pet may have
been sprayed by a skunk.
The stinky odor can keep
returning for weeks,
especially if it gets wet. The
bad smell is a wonderful
defense for a slow animal.
Only some birds of prey,
such as owls, will attack a

skunk. The smelly liquid is sprayed from glands under the tail and can be replaced in about one week. Young can spray as early as seven weeks. First the skunk will give a warning hiss, then stamp its feet, and finally arch its back and lift its tail to spray. It can shoot the liquid sixteen feet, but wind will take it farther. Yuck!

Stinkbug

Have you ever been weeding or picking berries and noticed a strong, smelly odor? You may have disturbed a stinkbug. As you might guess from its name, the stinkbug has glands on the middle segment of its body (thorax) that emit a bad-smelling liquid, helping to protect it from predators.

Skunk cabbage

In late February and early March you may see skunk cabbage leaves pushing up through swamp mud and snow. Through a process called thermogenesis, the plant's cells actually generate enough heat to melt snow. First to poke through the surface is a purple green hood surrounding a spongy spike (spadix) covered in small flowers. The flowers give off a skunklike odor with hints of decaying meat. We find the smell offensive, but, along with the warmth the plant gives off, the odor attracts gnats and flies for pollination. The hood gradually withers and giant leaves unfurl.

Fox

In late January, if you follow a fox's tracks and find where it has urinated, you will smell a strong, almost skunklike odor. It is only present in mating season. The smell can be blown quite a distance by the wind and is unmistakable.

Mystery solved!

Hmmm . . .
There's some fuzzy stuff that looks like poop at the bottom of that tree.

Who could have left it?

Let's look closely and find out.

Don't be repulsed. It might not be poop—it could be an owl pellet. Owls swallow their prey whole, but they can't digest bones, feathers, or fur. An owl's stomach compacts these parts into a blob called a pellet. The owl then throws up the pellet, which quickly dries.

By looking into the pellet you can figure out what the owl has eaten. Carefully pull it apart with your fingers or tweezers. If it is too hard you can soak it in water first. Be sure to wash your hands afterward.

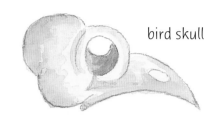
bird skull

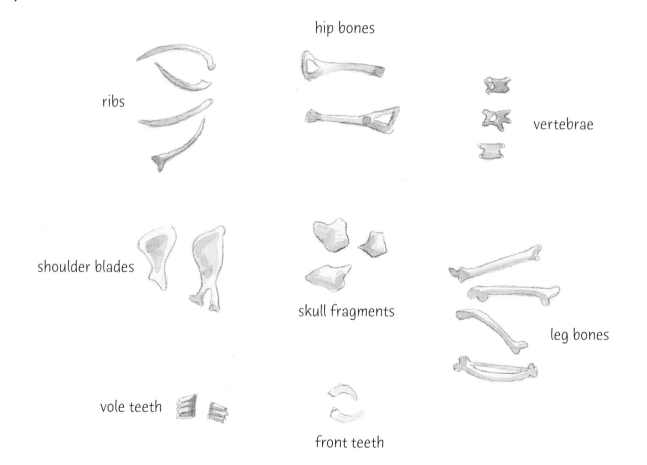

hip bones

ribs

vertebrae

shoulder blades

skull fragments

leg bones

vole teeth

front teeth

Mouse skull

Look for cheek teeth with small cusps  and long, curved, yellow front teeth.

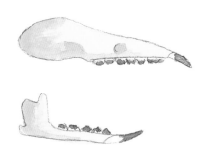

Shrew skull

Look for a narrow skull with reddish-tipped teeth.

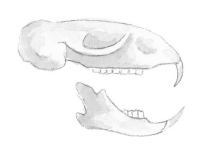

Vole skull

Cheek teeth "zigzag" when you view them from above. Long, yellow front teeth.

Mystery solved!

Hmmm . . .
There are footprints
in the snow.

Who was here before
you walked by? Let's look
closely and find out.

When you want to know what animals have been here, you can read their tracks like a newspaper.

a fox walks by (maybe smells the rabbit)

rabbit hops away

a pheasant lands

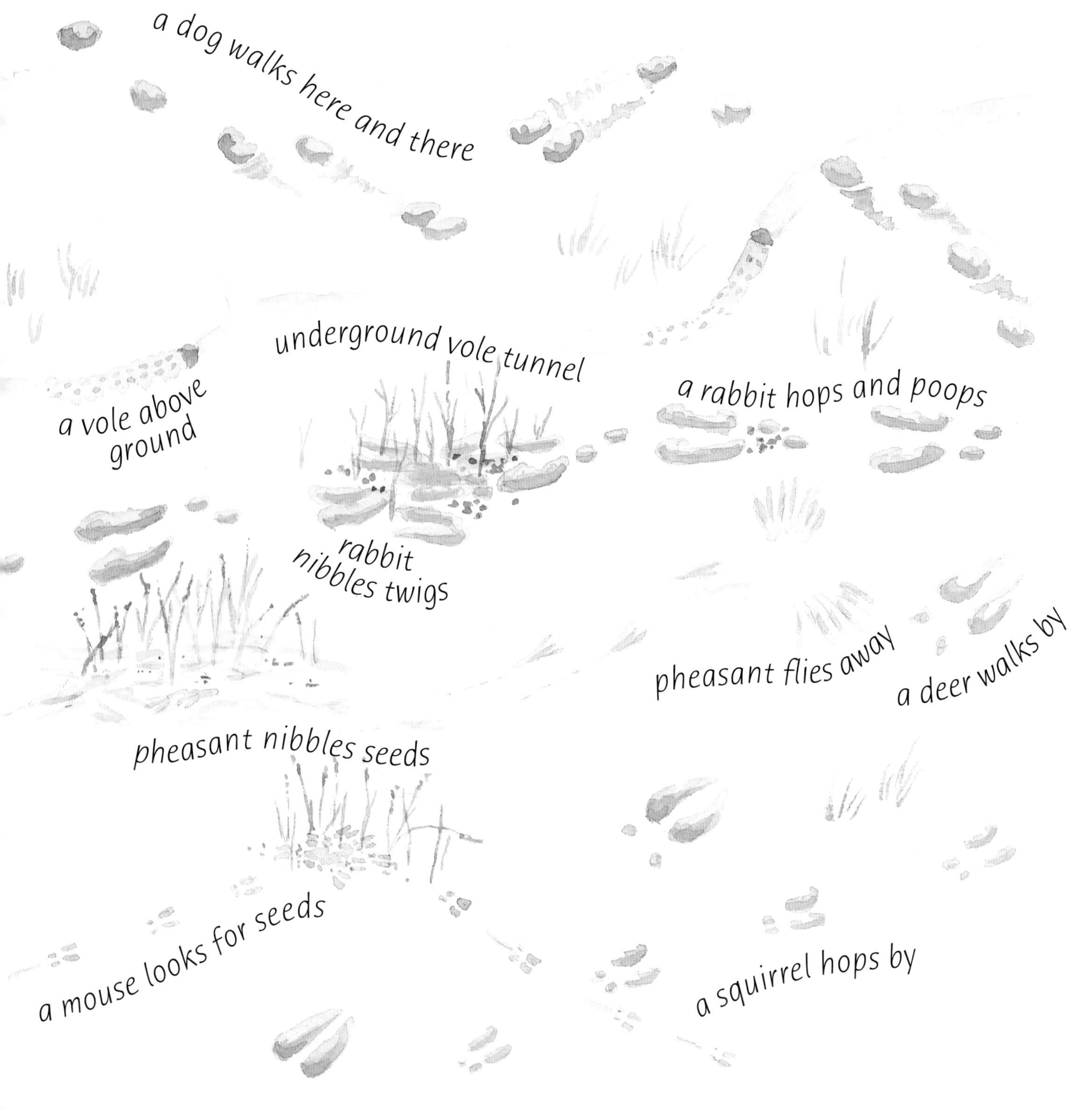

a dog walks here and there

underground vole tunnel

a vole above ground

a rabbit hops and poops

rabbit nibbles twigs

pheasant flies away

a deer walks by

pheasant nibbles seeds

a mouse looks for seeds

a squirrel hops by

35

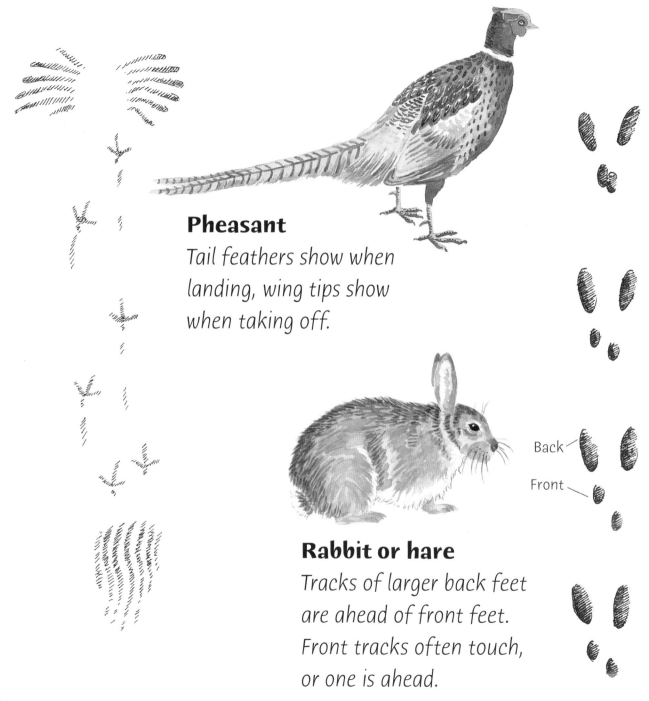

Pheasant

Tail feathers show when landing, wing tips show when taking off.

Rabbit or hare

Back

Front

Tracks of larger back feet are ahead of front feet. Front tracks often touch, or one is ahead.

Mouse

Usually a four-track pattern, smaller than a squirrel's, often with tail dragging.

Vole

Many tunnels under the snow connected by tiny double-print tracks on the surface.

Back —
Front —

Squirrel

Not as big as a rabbit's. Smaller front tracks are side by side, not touching.

Coyote

Tracks larger and rounder than fox's. Also in a straight line.

4 inches or less

4 to 6 inches

Fox

Very oval-shaped tracks. Hind track falls on front one, so trail is often a straight line.

Dog

Tracks rounder and toes more spread out than coyote's. Size varies. Trail wanders; irregular with foot drags.

Deer

Heart shaped. Small, round dewclaws show when running or in deep snow.

Raccoon

Often in pairs side by side. Look like small human hands and feet.

Cat

Small, neat, usually straight trail. Claws don't show.

Hmmm . . .
There
are some
marks in
the woods.

Who could
have left
them?

Let's look
closely and
find out.

Yellow-bellied sapsucker

This woodpecker bores holes in lines on tree trunks. It then uses its brushlike tongue to eat sap, as well as insects attracted to the sap.

Beaver

This rodent doesn't actually eat wood; it is after the living layers (cambium and phloem) of the inner bark. It does not climb, so chewing marks are found at the base of trees or branches on the ground, and often there are piles of wood chips.

41

Red squirrel

Strips winged seeds from pinecones. It eats the seeds, leaving piles of wings and clean shafts, often at the base of a favorite eating site.

Porcupine

Like the beaver, this rodent chews the inner bark (cambium and phloem) of tree trunks. But because it is a climber, unlike the beaver, you'll see its gnawing marks in the upper part of trees.

Woodpecker

Makes shallow holes in trees when seeking insects. Deeper holes can be either feeding or nesting cavities.

Deer

Feeds on woody twigs in winter. Because a deer has no upper front teeth, it holds the twig with its tongue and jerks its head to break it. The result is a ragged, torn cut.

Rabbit

Like deer, it feeds on woody twigs. But because it has upper and lower front teeth, when a rabbit bites a twig it leaves a neat, clean, 45-degree-angle cut.

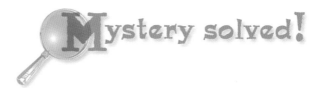

Hmmm . . .
There's a spider.

Why don't spiders stick
to their own webs?

Let's look closely
and find out.

45

Spider spinning a spiral orb web. Under the back end of its abdomen, tubes called spinnerets (silk glands) squirt out silk like toothpaste. When the silk hits the air it hardens.

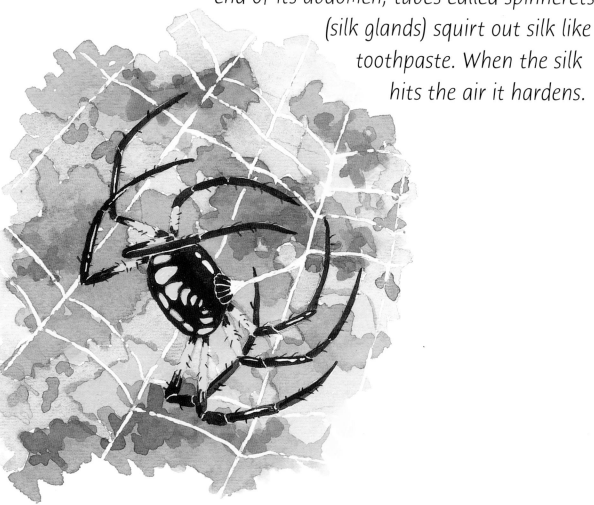

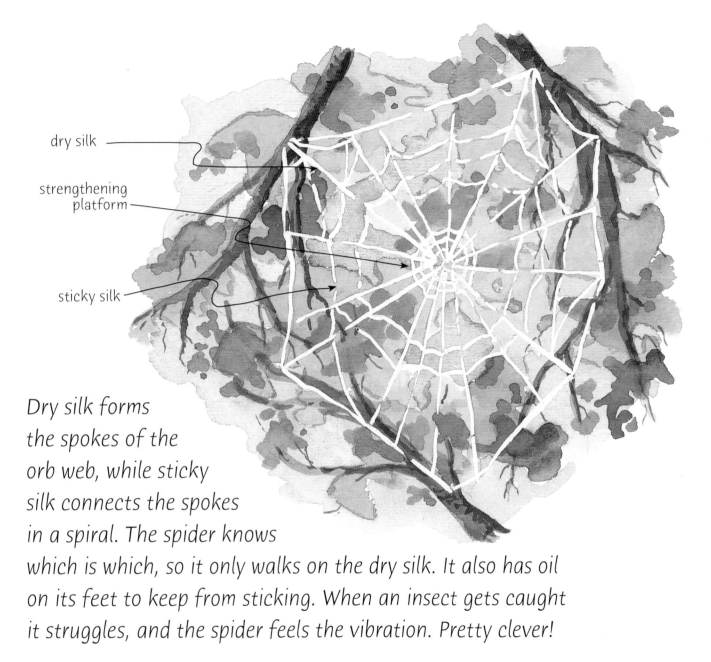

dry silk

strengthening platform

sticky silk

Dry silk forms
the spokes of the
orb web, while sticky
silk connects the spokes
in a spiral. The spider knows
which is which, so it only walks on the dry silk. It also has oil
on its feet to keep from sticking. When an insect gets caught
it struggles, and the spider feels the vibration. Pretty clever!

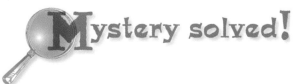

Mystery solved!

Hmmm . . . Suddenly there are mushrooms in the field when yesterday there were none.

Where did they come from?

Let's look closely and find out.

The reason mushrooms can appear overnight is that the main part of the fungus is already underground, unseen, in a network of tiny, tangled threads. The mushroom we see is the fruiting (reproductive) body, which pops up aboveground when the soil gets wet enough.

Mystery solved!

When a spore lands on damp soil, threads grow and branch. These threads take in water and food from the soil.

If the weather is damp or rainy, the button absorbs water and swells upward quickly.

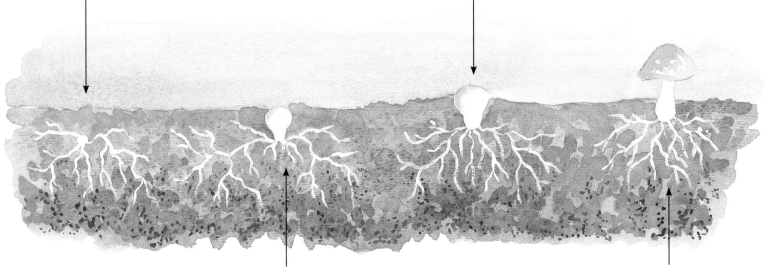

When the threads are large enough and humidity is right, a bump forms and swells into a button.

A mushroom can double in size in one day.

Northern oriole

Hanging pouch made of fibers, string, hair, bark strips.

Hmmm . . . There's a nest.

Do you know which bird built it?

Let's look closely and find out.

Hummingbird

Tiny cup (inside diameter less than 1 inch) made of fibers, down, and lichens; attached to branches with spiderwebs.

Barn swallow

Cup formed of layers of mud and straw attached to beams or eaves.

Chimney swift

Shallow cup of sticks glued together with saliva inside chimneys, trees, barns.

hairy:
    2 inches wide by 2½ inches high

flicker:
    2 to 4 inches wide

Woodpeckers

approximate hole size

downy:
    1¼-inch circle

pileated:
    3¼ inches wide by 3½ inches high

Catbird

In thickets, briars, and shrubs. Messy cup made of vines, leaves, twigs, and grass, lined with rootlets. Under 15 inches outside; 3 inches or less inside.

Ninety percent of nests found in the Northeast are cuplike and belong to the following birds: catbird, goldfinch, chipping sparrow, northern oriole, redstart, yellow warbler, song sparrow, red-eyed vireo, and robin.

Neat cup

goldfinch: lined with thistledown, wider than high; inside diameter 2 inches

redstart: no down lining, higher than wide, thin walls; inside diameter 1¾ inches

yellow warbler: often lined with milkweed down, higher than wide, thick walls; inside diameter 1¾ to 2 inches

Red-eyed vireo

Deep cup hanging below horizontal branches. Built of grass, bark strips, and rootlets; outside has spiderwebs and lichens. Less than 2 inches deep.

Robin

In shrubs and trees, on ledges. Deep cup, mainly grasses worked into mud. Inside diameter under 4 inches.

Sparrow

Mostly made of grass and rootlets, usually with horsehair in the cup lining.

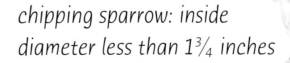

chipping sparrow: inside diameter less than $1\frac{3}{4}$ inches

song sparrow: inside diameter over 2 inches

Mystery solved!

Hmmm . . .

There are some little
holes in the ground.

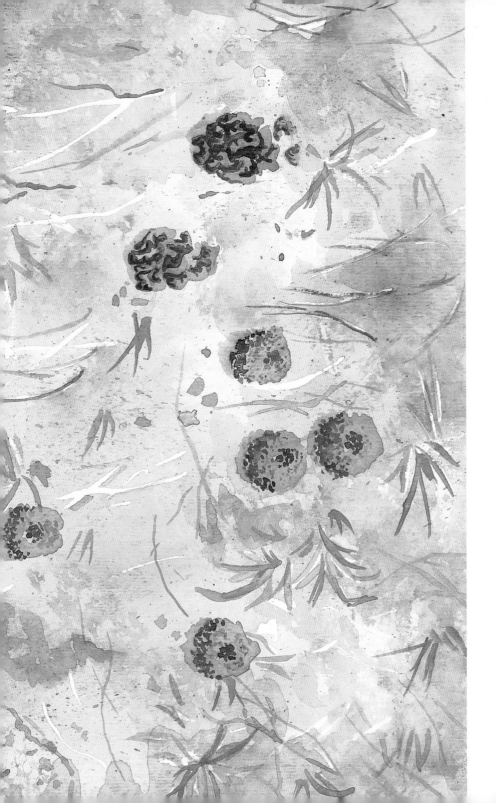

Do you know
what might have
made them?

Let's look closely
and find out.

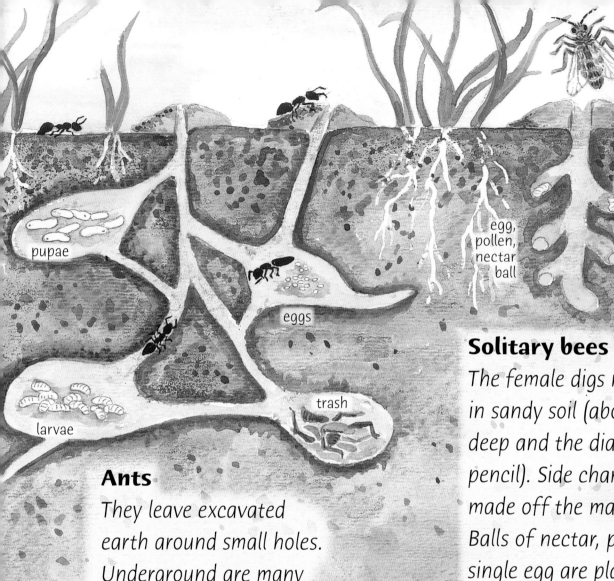

pupae

eggs

larvae

trash

larvae

egg,
pollen,
nectar
ball

Ants

They leave excavated earth around small holes. Underground are many tunnels branching into rooms for eggs, larvae, pupae, food, and trash.

Solitary bees

The female digs nest tunnels in sandy soil (about 1 foot deep and the diameter of a pencil). Side chambers are made off the main tunnel. Balls of nectar, pollen, and a single egg are placed inside each chamber so the larvae have food when they hatch. After pupating, the young emerge from the burrow as adults in late summer.

58

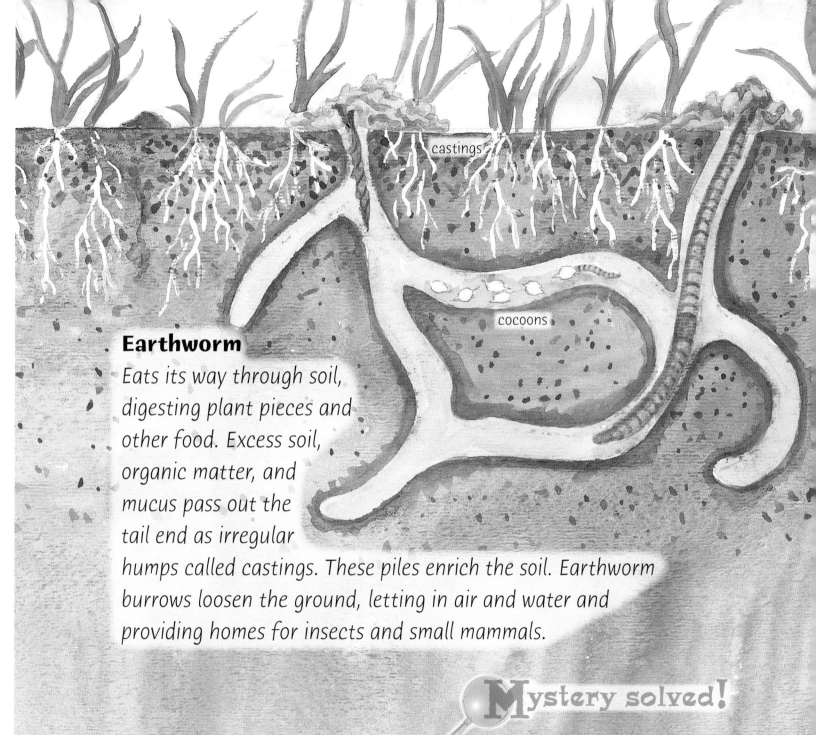

castings

cocoons

Earthworm

Eats its way through soil, digesting plant pieces and other food. Excess soil, organic matter, and mucus pass out the tail end as irregular humps called castings. These piles enrich the soil. Earthworm burrows loosen the ground, letting in air and water and providing homes for insects and small mammals.

Mystery solved!

Fun Things to Do in Nature

Spittlebug
Peek inside some spittle and look for different-sized nymphs. Remember to cover the spittlebugs back up with foam when you are done.

Colored leaves
Tear up a green leaf, put the pieces into a glass, cover them with rubbing alcohol, and mash them. Cut a 2-by-4-inch strip from a coffee filter and tape one end to a pencil. Lay the pencil across the top of the glass so the bottom of the strip reaches the liquid. When the liquid moves halfway up the strip, remove and let dry. You should see color bands—green for chlorophyll and yellow for carotenoids. The alcohol has separated the pigments.

Spiderwebs
Find an abandoned web and spray it with paint. Then have an adult spray it with a varnish or fixative (avoid breathing the fumes). Take stiff paper and slowly lay the web on it, cutting the attachments gently (it might be easier to have a second person help). Once the web is on the paper, spray again with varnish to hold it. Now you have a real web you can frame.

Smells
Using a small net, sweep through long grass looking for a stinkbug. You'll know you've found one by the stink. Look at it, sniff, and let it go. You may need to wash your hands if they get smelly.

Butterflies
Hang a butterfly feeder (with sugar water and rotting fruit) and watch. Or plant a butterfly garden—the right flowers will attract butterflies to your yard.

Frog calls
Visit a pond some evening and count how many different calls you can hear. Try to copy some. If you can't get to a frog pond, go to a Web site like www.allaboutfrogs.org/weird/general/songs.html to hear different frog calls.

Forest marks
Next time you go into the woods, look up and around at the trees and shrubs and see what marks and holes you can find.

Footprints

If you can't find any wild animal tracks, follow your dog or cat in the snow or mud. You should be able to tell when it walks, runs, and stops to sniff around.

Bird nest

Try to make a nest yourself. Find some grass, vines, string, or twigs; with the help of a little mud or clay, form a small cup. It is harder than you think—even with hands. You can line your nest with feathers or grass and let it dry.

Mushrooms

Pick a wild mushroom and carefully cut off the stem. Place the top, gill side down, on white paper, or on dark paper if the spores are white. (If you can't tell whether spores are white or black, try putting mushrooms on both dark and light paper.) Cover with a bowl to protect from air currents. It's a good idea to wash your hands after handling wild mushrooms. Check the paper the next day. You should have a beautiful spore print. Gently spray with fixative and frame.

Owl pellet

If you can find a pellet, gently pull it apart. You'll know what the owl has been eating if you can identify the bones.

Ground holes

Find an anthill. Put down some cookie crumbs near the hole and watch the ants take them to the nest. Ants leave a scent trail for others to follow to the crumbs. If you erase part of the trail (sweep away some dirt), it will take a little while for them to find the crumbs again.

Glossary

abdomen. The part of the body containing the stomach and intestines. In an insect it is the third segment of the body, behind the thorax.

anthocyanin. A pigment that gives shades of red, as well as purple or blue, to plants.

cambium. The layer of cells just beneath tree bark that produces new trunk growth.

castings. Irregular humps of soil and organic matter left by earthworms.

chlorophyll. The green pigment in plants that uses the energy of sunlight, carbon dioxide, and water to create oxygen and simple sugars.

cocoon. A protective case, usually of silk, made by an insect larva before pupating.

fungus. A plantlike organism, such as a mushroom, that lacks chlorophyll and reproduces by spores.

larva (plural larvae). The immature stage, between egg and pupa, of most insects, amphibians, and fish; a larva does not resemble the adult (for example, caterpillar and butterfly, or tadpole and frog). An insect larva pupates while transforming into the adult stage.

nymph. The immature stage, between egg and adult, of some insects, such as spittlebugs and stinkbugs; a nymph resembles the adult stage and molts rather than pupates.

phloem. Food-conducting tissues of vascular plants; in trees the phloem is the inner layer of bark.

photosynthesis. The process by which plants use chlorophyll, carbon dioxide, and water to change energy from sunlight into food energy for themselves.

pigment. A substance that creates color in the tissues of plants and animals. *See* **chlorophyll** and **anthocyanin**.

pollen. The male spores of a plant, appearing as a fine powder in the center of a flower.

pollination. The process of transferring pollen from one flower to another, enabling the plant to reproduce; pollination is most often done by insects.

predator. An animal that hunts and kills other animals for food.

pupa (plural pupae). The stage between larva and adult in most insects; the pupa is enclosed in a protective case and remains stationary until emerging as an adult.

pupate. To go through the pupal stage.

spinneret. One of the tubes on the back end of a spider that squirts out silk; silk gland.

thermogenesis. The production of heat.

thorax. The middle segment of an insect's body, between the head and the abdomen; the legs and wings attach to the thorax.

toxic. Poisonous.

vacuole. A small cavity in a cell containing water, food, or waste.

About the Author

Peggy Kochanoff graduated from Cornell University with a degree in vertebrate zoology and spent a summer working at the Central Park Zoo in New York City. Eventually she settled with her husband and two sons (now grown) on a tree farm in Nova Scotia, Canada—a perfect place to combine her love of nature with art. She has done illustrations for nature trail brochures, a migratory bird storyboard, a nature series in the newspaper, animal calendars, and murals, as well as pet portraits and nature paintings. Mountain Press published her first two nature books, which were filled with pen-and-ink drawings. Her most recent book, *There's a Beagle in My Bed*, was a labor of love: her oldest son wrote it, she illustrated it, and it was about her granddaughter and granddog. Retiring from the farm has left more time to kayak, swim, bird-watch, ski, and draw. She is eager to teach her granddaughter all about the fun of nature.

Suggested Resources

For a list of scientific names of the species featured in this book, visit www.mountain-press.com.

Books

Field Guide to Nearby Nature: Fields and Woods of the Midwest and East Coast. P. Kochanoff. 1994. Missoula, MT: Mountain Press.

A Guide to Amphibians and Reptiles (Stokes Nature Guides). T. F. Tyning. 1990. New York: Little, Brown and Co.

Kaufman Field Guide to Insects of North America. E. R. Eaton and K. Kaufman. 2007. Boston: Houghton Mifflin.

Last Child in the Woods: Saving Our Children From Nature-Deficit Disorder. R. Louv. 2008. Algonquin Books.

National Geographic Field Guide to Birds of North America. J. L. Dunn and J. Alderfer. 2006. Washington, DC: National Geographic Society.

National Wildlife Federation Field Guide to Insects and Spiders of North America. A. V. Evans. 2007. New York: Sterling Publishing.

Peterson Field Guide to Animal Tracks. O. J. Murie and M. Elbrock. 2005. Boston: Houghton Mifflin.

Peterson Field Guide to Birds of North America. R. T. Peterson. 2008. Boston: Houghton Mifflin.

Peterson Field Guide to Eastern Birds' Nests. H. H. Harrison. 1998. Boston: Houghton Mifflin.

Peterson Field Guide to Mammals of North America. F. Reid. 2006. Boston: Houghton Mifflin.

Stokes Nature Guide to Animal Tracking and Behavior. D. Stokes and L. Stokes. 1987. New York: Little, Brown and Co.

The Sibley Guide to Birds. D. A. Sibley. 2000. New York: Alfred A. Knopf.

Tracking and the Art of Seeing: How to Read Animal Tracks and Signs. P. Rezendes. 1999. New York: Collins.

Nature Books for Kids

Caterpillars (Peterson Field Guide for Young Naturalists). J. P. Latimer, et al. 2000. Boston: Houghton Mifflin.

Fun with Nature (Take Along Guide). M. Boring. 1998. New York: NorthWord Books.

The Kids' Nature Book: 365 Indoor/ Outdoor Activities and Experiences. S. Milord. 1996. Charlotte, VT: Williamson Publishing.

My Nature Journal: A Personal Nature Guide for Young People. A. Olmstead. 1999. Lafayette, CA: Pajaro.

Nature Ranger (DK Nature Activities). D. Burnie. 2006. New York: DK Children.

Nature's Yucky: Gross Stuff That Helps Nature Work. L. Landstrom and K. Shragg. 2003. Missoula, MT: Mountain Press.

Owl Puke. J. Hammerslough. 2004. New York: Workman Publishing.

Peterson First Guide to Forests. J. C. Kricher. 1999. Boston: Houghton Mifflin.

Peterson First Guide to Insects of North America. C. Leahy. 1998. Boston: Houghton Mifflin.

Peterson First Guide to Reptiles and Amphibians. R. Conant. 1999. Boston: Houghton Mifflin.

Smithsonian Bird-Watcher (DK Nature Activities). D. Burnie. 2005. New York: DK Publishing.

Under One Rock: Bugs, Slugs, and Other Ughs (Sharing Nature with Children Book). A. Fredericks. 2001. Nevada City, CA: Dawn Publications.

Magazines for Kids

National Geographic Kids
National Wildlife
Ranger Rick
Wild
Your Big Backyard

Web Sites

Canadian Wildlife Federation: *www.cwf-fcf.org*

Cornell Lab of Ornithology: *www.birds.cornell.edu*

Frogland: *www.allaboutfrogs.org*

National Geographic for Kids: *www.kids.nationalgeographic.com*

National Wildlife Federation: *www.nwf.org*

Ranger Rick's Green Zone: *www.nwf.org/rrgreenzone*

Robert Bateman's "Get to Know" Program (connecting youth to nature): *www.gettoknow.ca*

WonderQuest: *www.wonderquest.com*